Handy Arizona Genealogy Handbook

I0441265

Gary L. Morris

ISBN-13:978-1505359732
ISBN-10:1505359732

Table of Contents

Genealogical Research in Arizona

Tracing ancestry has become a popular hobby in the state of Arizona, as many residents of the state are attempting to piece together family trees to pass down through generations. If you need help finding your ancestry, on this page we will introduce you to those records, and help you to understand:

1. What they are
2. Where to find them
3. How to use them
4.

These records can be found both online and off, so we'll introduce you to online websites, indexes and databases, as well as brick-and-mortar repositories and other institutions that will help with your research in Arizona. So that you will have a more comprehensive understanding of these records, we have provided a brief history of the "Copper State"to illustrate what type of records may have been generated during specific time periods. That information will assist you in pinpointing times and locations on which to focus the search for your Arizona ancestors.

A Brief History of Arizona

The first Europeans arrived in the Arizona region in 1539 when Marcos de Niza explored the area. The Spanish continued to hold an interest in Arizona until 1821 when Arizona became part of Mexico. After the Mexican-American War from 1846-1848, the United States took possession, although the area was attached to the then Territory of New Mexico.

In 1863 Arizona became its own entity, and the development of railroads hastened its growth. Statehood was granted to Arizona in 1912, and at that time the economy revolved around the growth of cotton and citrus, cattle rearing, and the mining of copper. Arizona became the largest producer of copper in America while developing gold, silver, lead, and uranium mines. In later years the dry, warm climate attracted retired persons and those seeking to improve their health; while in modern times the state has become somewhat of a golfing Mecca.

Important Genealogical Dates in Arizona History

- **1629** – Franciscan monks establish first missions in northeastern Arizona.
- **1692** – The Jesuits establish missions in the southeast part of the state.
- **1726** – Spanish settlers found Tubac.
- **1776** - First Spanish settlement established at Tucson.
- **1821** – Becomes part of Mexico
- **1846** – Mormon battalion opens Cooke's Wagon Road to California.
- **1848** – Acquired from Mexico after Mexican-American War.
- **1850** – Becomes part of New Mexico Territory.
- **1862** – Confederate Congress establishes Territory of Arizona
- **1863** – Organized by Congress into a separate territory.
- **1910** – Adopted the U.S. Constitution.
- **1912** – Statehood Granted

Famous Battles Fought in Arizona

Many battles were fought to win the territory now known as Arizona. In addition to the Mexican-American War and the Civil War, many battles were waged with the Native Americans who inhabited the land. The men who fought in the armies of Arizona developed stellar reputations as fighters and fought in the Spanish-American War, and were sent to Mexico to assist in quelling the violence during the Mexican Revolution.

The information contained in accounts and other documentation of famous battles can be very effective in uncovering the military records of your ancestor. They can tell you what regiments fought in which battles, and often include the names and ranks of many officers and enlisted men. Following are some of the most famous battles fought in Arizona and links to useful information about them.

Battle of Picacho Peak (Picacho Pass), 1862
http://www.civilwar.org/battlefields/picachopeak.html

Arizona Apache Wars (1846-1886)
http://zybtarizona.com/awars.htm

Mexican War (1846-1848)
http://zybtarizona.com/mwar.htm

Civil War Battles
https://edgeinducedcohesion.wordpress.com/2012/03/03/arizona-a-forgotten-theater-of-the-civil-war/

Common Arizona Genealogical Issues and Resources to Overcome Them

Boundary Changes: A common obstacle when researching Arizona ancestors are historical boundary changes. You could be searching for an ancestor's record in one county when in fact it is stored in a different one due to historical county boundary changes. The **Atlas of Historical County Boundaries** can help you to overcome that problem. It provides a chronological listing of every boundary change that has occurred in the history of Arizona.

Atlas of Historical County Boundaries
http://publications.newberry.org/ahcbp/documents/AZ_Consolidated_Chronology.htm#Consolidated_Chronology

Name Changes: Surname changes, variations, and misspellings can complicate genealogical research. It is important to check all spelling variations. Soundex, a program that indexes names by sound, is a useful first step, but you can't rely on it completely as some name variations result in different Soundex codes. The surnames could be different, but the first name may be different too. You can also find records filed under initials, middle names, and nicknames as well, so you will need to get creative with surname variations and spellings in order to cover all the possibilities. For help with surname variations read our instructional article on **How to Use Soundex**.

How to Use Soundex: http://obituarieshelp.org/blog/?p=505

Arizona Genealogical Organizations and Archives

Genealogical resources include not only records, but the organizations that house them, or can direct you to them. These institutions include: *Archives, Libraries, Genealogical Societies, Family History Centers, Universities, Churches, and Museums.*

Following are links to their websites, their physical addresses, and a summary of the records you can find there.

Archives

Arizona Department of Health Services – Birth and death certificates

Arizona Department of Health Services
150 North 18th Avenue
Phoenix, Arizona 85007
Tel: (602) 542-1025
Fax: (602) 542-0883

Website: http://genealogy.az.gov/

Arizona State Library – court records, historical newspapers, maps, books, periodicals, family and community histories, genealogical journals

State Library of Arizona
1700 W. Washington Suite 300
Phoenix, AZ 85007
Tel: 602-926-3870
Fax: 602-256-7984

Website: http://www.azlibrary.gov/is/genealogy/#premium

US National Archives – Census reports, immigration records, land records, court records, slave records, military records, and naturalization records

New Mexico State Records Center and Archives

State Records Center and Archives
1205 Camino Carlos Rey
Santa Fe, NM 87507

Website: http://www.archives.gov/research/genealogy/index.html

Arizona Genealogical and Historical Societies

Genealogical and historical societies have access to extensive catalogues of genealogical data. They are also able to offer expert guidance for genealogical researchers. Many members are professional genealogists who are most willing to share their expertise in finding ancestors.

Arizona Branch National Society Sons & Daughters of the Pilgrims

Georgia Hier
56244 W. McDavid
Maricopa, AZ 85139
Email: azhier@cox.net

Arizona Historical Society – manuscript collection, historical photographs, oral histories, maps, historical books

Website: http://www.arizonahistoricalsociety.org/

Arizona Division Sons of Confederate Veterans – Civil War records, grave registry, historical documents

Website:
http://home.earthlink.net/~cssscv/arizonadivisionsonsofconfederatev eterans/id32.html

Arizona Society Daughters of the American Revolution – biographies, histories, genealogies, directories, manuscripts, periodicals, Native American records, bible records, cemetery records, military records

37231 S. Pinewood Dr.
SaddleBrooke
Arizona 85739-1040
Email: dannaepdar@wbhsi.net

Arizona Society Daughters of the American Revolution link to:
http://www.arizonadar.org/

Black Family Genealogy & History Society – biographies, listing of African American pioneers who died in Arizona before and after statehood.

P. O. Box 90683
Phoenix, Arizona 85066-0683

Website: http://www.bfghs.com/AZAAPioneers.htm

Genealogical Society of Yuma Arizona – cemetery records, historical newspapers, research assistance

P.O. Box 2905
Yuma, AZ 85366-2905

Website: http://www.gsya.org/

Huguenot Society of Arizona – historical and religious records of the Huguenots in Arizona

P. O. Box 1412
Chino Valley, AZ 86323-1412
Tel: 928-636-2489

Website: http://huguenot.netnation.com/general/

Phoenix Genealogical Society

P.O. Box 38703
Phoenix, Arizona 85069-8703
Tel: 602-687-7030
Email: phxgensociety@gmail.com

Website: http://www.rootsweb.ancestry.com/~azpgs/

Family History Society of Arizona – cemetery records and huge surname database searchable online

Website: http://fhsa.org/surnames.phtml

Arizona Family History Centers

The Family History Centers run by the LDS Church offer free access to billions of genealogical records for free to the general public. They also provide classes on genealogy and one-on-one assistance to inexperienced family historians. Here you will find a **Complete Listing of Arizona Family History Centers**.

Complete Listing of Arizona Family History Centers:
https://familysearch.org/locations/centerlocator

Additional Arizona Genealogical Resources

Arizona Mailing Lists

Mailing lists are internet based facilities that use email to distribute a single message to all who subscribe to it. When information on a particular surname, new records, or any other important genealogy information related to the mailing list topic becomes available, the subscribers are alerted to it. Joining a mailing list is an excellent way to stay up to date on Arizona genealogy research topics. Rootsweb have an extensive listing of **Arizona Mailing Lists** on a variety of topics.

Arizona Mailing Lists:
http://lists.rootsweb.ancestry.com/index/usa/AZ/misc.html

Arizona Message Boards

A message board is another internet based facility where people can post questions about a specific genealogy topic and have it answered by other genealogists. If you have questions about a surname, record type, or research topic, you can post your question and other researchers and genealogists will help you with the answer. You must make sure to check back regularly, as the answers are not emailed to you. The message boards at the **Arizona Genealogy Forum** are completely free to use.

Arizona Genealogy Forum: http://genforum.genealogy.com/az/

<u>Arizona Newspapers and Periodicals</u>

Many genealogy periodicals and historical newspapers contain reprinted copies of family genealogies, transcripts of family Bible records, information about local records and archives, census indexes, church records, queries, land records, obituaries, court records, cemetery records, and wills. **Arizona State University Libraries** have an extensive collection of historical newspapers and periodicals.

Arizona State University Libraries:
http://libguides.asu.edu/content.php?pid=6321&sid=751348

<u>Historical Arizona Maps and Gazetteers</u>

Maps are an integral part of genealogical research. They help us to locate landmarks, towns, cities, parishes, states, provinces, waterways and roads and streets. They also help us to determine when and where boundary changes might have taken place, and give us a visualization of the area we're researching in. For locating place names, a gazetteer is the best possible resource for any genealogist. Gazetteers are also sometimes called "place name dictionaries", and can help you to locate the area in which you need to conduct research. Below are links to the maps and gazetteers for research in Arizona.

Peabody GNIS Service – Arizona:
http://peabody.research.yale.edu/cgi-bin/Query.GNIS?ST=Arizona&SU=1

Color Landform Atlas – Arizona:
http://fermi.jhuapl.edu/states/az_0.html

1985 U.S. Atlas: http://www.livgenmi.com/1895/AZ/

Arizona Hometown Locator: http://arizona.hometownlocator.com/

Arizona Genealogical Records

Birth, Death, Marriage and Divorce Records – Birth, death, and marriage records are the most basic, yet most important records attached to your ancestor. They are generally referred to as vital records as they record vital life events. The reason for their importance is that they not only place your ancestor in a specific place at a definite time, but potentially connect the individual to other relatives. Below is a list of repositories where you can find Arizona vital records

Arizona Department of Health Services – Birth and death certificates

Arizona Department of Health Services: http://genealogy.az.gov/

Arizona marriage and divorce records are maintained by the **Clerk of the Superior Court** in the county where the event occurred.

Clerk of the Superior Court:
http://www.azcourts.gov/azcourts/azcourtslocator.aspx

Census Reports

Census records are among the most important genealogical documents for placing your ancestor in a particular place at a specific time. Like BDM records, they can also lead you to other ancestors, particularly those who were living under the authority of the head of household.

Official Arizona census records exist from 1831-1940 and many images and indexes can be viewed online. Following are the best places to find Arizona census records.

U.S National Archives – Federal census records on microfilm available from 1790 to 1940.

U.S National Archives: http://www.archives.gov/research/census/

Internet Archive – schedules from 1860-1930

Internet Archive link to: http://archive.org/search.php?query=arizona%20census%20records

FamilyLink.com - 1860-1930 census schedules

FamilyLink.com: http://www.familylink.com/contentsearch.aspx?p=Arizona

Arizona Church Records

Church and synagogue records are a valuable resource, especially for baptisms, marriages, and burials that took place before 1900. There are a few challenges to locating and accessing church records, such as the multitude of religious denominations that exist. Once found however, they can reveal information about your ancestor that other records do not. You will need to at least have an idea of your ancestor's religious denomination, and in most cases you will have to visit a brick and mortar establishment to view them. Below are links archives that maintain church records, as well as a few databases that can be viewed online.

The **Family History Library** has an extensive collection of LDS church records. The library has histories of local Latter Day Saint congregations and an overview of Mormon colonization in Arizona.

Family History Library:
http://familysearch.org/learn/wiki/en/Family_History_Library

Presbyterian Historical Society

United Presbyterian Church in the United States
425 Lombard Street
Philadelphia, PA 19147
Tel: (215) 627-1852
Fax: (215) 627-0509

Website: http://www.history.pcusa.org/

Diocese of Phoenix Archives (Roman Catholic)

400 East Monroe St.
Phoenix, AZ 85004
Tel: (602) 354-2475

Includes the counties of Maricopa, Mohave, Coconino, and Yavapai

Website: http://www.diocesephoenix.org/index.php

Diocese of Tucson Archives (Roman Catholic)

300 S. Tucson Blvd.
Tucson, AZ 85716
Tel: (520) 886-5201

The diocese includes the counties of: Graham, Greenlee, Cochise, Gila, Pima, Pinal, La Paz, Santa Cruz and Yuma

Website:
http://www.diocesetucson.org/Archives%20website/archiveindex.ht m

The counties of Apache and Navajo are included in the **Diocese of Gallup, New Mexico**.

Website: http://www.dioceseofgallup.org/

The **Arizona Historical Society** maintains early Spanish Catholic Church records in its collections.

Website: http://www.arizonahistoricalsociety.org/

Arizona Military Records

More than 40 million Americans have participated in some time of war service since America was colonized. The chance of finding your ancestor amongst those records is exceptionally high. Military records can even reveal individuals who never actually served, such as those who registered for the two World Wars but were never called to duty.Below are a number of links to websites and archives that contain Arizona military records.

U.S. National Archives – WWI Draft registration cards, casualties lists, WWI and WWII service records, Korean War records, Vietnam War records, Civil War and Spanish-American War records, and casualties lists.

Website:
http://www.archives.gov/research/military/veterans/online.html

US Department of Veterans Affairs Nationwide Gravesite Locator – includes information on veterans and their family members buried in veterans and military cemeteries having a government grave marker.

US Department of Veterans Affairs Nationwide Gravesite Locator: http://gravelocator.cem.va.gov/

United States Mexican War Pension Index, 1887-1926 - Mexican War pension files

United States Mexican War Pension Index, 1887-1926:
https://familysearch.org/search/collection/1979390

Civil War Soldiers Service Records - Service records for both Union and Confederate soldiers indexed by soldier's name, rank, and unit.

Civil War Soldier Service Records:
http://go.fold3.com/civilwar_records/

Arizona Cemetery Records

As convenient as it is to search cemetery records online, keep in mind that there are a few disadvantages over visiting a cemetery in person. They are:

- Tombstone information is not always accurately transcribed
- The arrangement of the graves in a cemetery can be crucial as family members are often buried next to each other or in the same grave. This arrangement is not always preserved in the alphabetical indexes that are found online.

With that information in mind, the following websites have databases that can be searched online for Arizona Cemetery records.

Arizona Gravestone Photo Project - tombstone photographs and burial information

Arizona Gravestone Photo Project: http://arizonagravestones.org/

Find a Grave – over 100 million grave records can be searched on this site. Search can be conducted by name, location, or cemetery name.

Find a Grave: http://www.findagrave.com/

Interment.net - A free online database containing approximately 4 million cemetery records from around the world.

Interment.net link to: http://www.interment.net/

Arizona Tombstone Transcription Project - death and burial records

Arizona Tombstone Transcription Project:
http://usgwtombstones.org/arizona/arizona.html

Billion Graves – as the name implies, you can search a billion records including headstone photos, transcriptions, cemetery records, and grave locations.

Billion Graves :
http://billiongraves.com/pages/search/index.php#cemetery

Arizona Obituaries

Obituaries can reveal a wealth about our ancestor and other relatives. You can search our **Arizona Newspaper Obituaries Listings** from hundreds of Arizona newspapers online for free.

Arizona Newspaper Obituaries Listings link to:
http://obituarieshelp.org/arizona_newspaper_obituaries.html

Arizona Wills and Probate Records

Arizona probate records were kept by the New Mexico probate courts during the territorial period of 1850 to 1864. The Arizona county probate courts then maintained files for estate dispositions until 1912. They are now handled by the **Superior Court** in individual counties where you can find wills, claims, case files, calendars, and administrations.

The documents found in a probate packet may include a complete inventory of a person's estate, newspaper entries, witness testimony, a copy of a will, list of debtors and creditors, names of executors or trustees, names of heirs. They can not only tell you about the ancestor you're currently researching, but lead to other ancestors. Most of these records must be accessed at a county court or clerk's office, but some can be found online as well.

Superior Court:
http://www.azcourts.gov/AZCourts/SuperiorCourt.aspx

Arizona Immigration and Naturalization Records

The naturalization process generated many types of records, including petitions, declarations of intention, and oaths of allegiance. These records can provide family historians with information such as a person's birth date and place of birth, immigration year, marital status, spouse information, occupation, witnesses' names and addresses, and more.

The US National Archives at Riverside holds these records for Arizona. They include certificates of citizenship, petitions for naturalizations, indexes to county naturalization records, declarations of intent, and certificates of naturalization dating from 1864.

The US National Archives at Riverside:
http://www.archives.gov/riverside/finding-aids/naturalization-records.html

The late 19th and early 20th centuries saw many Mexicans crossing into Arizona. These **Mexican Border Crossing Records** are also available at the National Archives

Mexican Border Crossing Records:
http://www.archives.gov/research/immigration/border-mexico.html

The **Arizona County Histories** at FamilySearch.org contain much information about ethnic groups which settled in that county.

Arizona County Histories link to:
http://familysearch.org/learn/wiki/en/Arizona

Arizona City Directories

City directories are similar to telephone directories in that they list the residents of a particular area. The difference though is what is important to genealogists, and that is they pre-date telephone directories. You can find an ancestor's information such as their street address, place of employment, occupation, or the name of their spouse. A one-stop-shop for finding city directories in Arizona is the **Arizona Online Historical Directories** which contains a listing of every available city and historical directory related to Arizona.

Arizona Online Historical Directories link to:
https://sites.google.com/site/onlinedirectorysite/Home/usa/az

Missing Matriarchs – Resources for Researching Female Arizona Ancestors

Looking for female ancestors requires an adjustment of how we view traditional records sources. A woman's identity was often under that of her husband, and often individual records for them can be difficult to locate. The following resources are effective in locating female ancestors in Arizona where traditional records may not reveal them.

Marriage and Divorce Records

1. University of Arizona Tucson – Early Catholic parish registers, 1793-1849 on microfilm
2. Arizona Historical Society – Parish registers 1768-1825 on microfilm
3. Arizona State Archive – marriage records 1871-1942 microfilm (film 1955594 ff.)

Native American Records

The **National Archives** - information about American Indians who maintained their ties to Federally-recognized Tribes (1830-1970).

National Archives: http://www.archives.gov/research/native-americans/

Bureau of Indian Affairs: http://www.bia.gov/

Bibliographies

1. *Ladies, Livestock, Land and the Lucre: Women's Networks and Social Status on the Western Navajo Reservation*, Christine Conte, American Indian Quarterly 6, 1982, pages 105-24
2. *Arizona Women's Hall of Fame* – Arizona Historical Society
3. *Desert Documentary: The Spanish Years, 1767-1821*, Kiernan McCarly, Arizona Historical Society

4. *Take up Your Mission: Mormon Colonizing Along the Little Colorado River, 1870-1900*, Charles S. Peterson, University of Arizona Press, 1973
5. *Genealogical Guide to Arizona and Nevada,* Joyce V. Hawley, Verlene Publishing, 1963

Selected Resources for Arizona Women's History

Arizona Department of Library, Archives, and Public Records
1700 West Washington
Phoenix, AZ 85007

Arizona Historical Society Library
1242 North Central Ave.
Phoenix, AZ 85004

University of Arizona Southwest Institute for Research on Women
102 Douglas Building
Tucson, AZ 85721

Common Arizona Surnames

The following surnames are among the most common in Arizona. The list is by no means exhaustive. If your surname doesn't appear in the list it doesn't mean that you have no Arizona connections, only that your surname may be less common.

Adamson, Akin, Alberta, Alice, Baldwin, Bauer, Belcher, Berger, Bergess, Betty, Beymia, Blue, Bolin, Bosen, Bourland, Brewer, Brorby, Burke, Carmack, Carrel, Cawvey, Chacon, Cheek, Children, Chistie, Clawson, Clover, Coffee, Daniels, Darlus, Delisle, Dobbs, Donna, Dortch, Doyle, Eaton, Elizabeth, Emma, Enlow, Epps, Fischer, Foster, Gabbin, Gablin, Gallardo, Galvan, Garcia, Garica, Gibbs, Gibson, Gieseking, Giovando, Grim, Gutterman, Haller, Harrington, Helen, Helfenstein, Holloway, Hopper, Irvin, Jenkins, Johnson, Judy, Keffer, Knebel, Kock, Kunkel, L., Lacy, Lamb, Lilley, Lillie, Long, Lore, Ludwig, Lukitich, Manley, Manuel, Martin, Mary, Mattado, Michelle, Milka, Miller, Morin, Nancy, Navaria, Oradell, Ortega, Osborn, Parsons, Patty, Pelate, Pocheck, Pollock, Ramon, Rawlins, Rayhart, Reed, Rhodes, Riddling, Ridling, Rodes, Romans, Sambrano, Sara, Schwartz, Sexton, Singleton, Sis, Sittles, Sleater, Smith, Sophia, Spinner, Stanley, Tanner, Theasa, Thornton, Thurston, Tremble, Tucker, Vallino, Wall, Wallheimer, Walton, Weathers, Weaver, Weikel, Whitlow, Wilds, Williams, Wilson, Zoller

www.ingramcontent.com/pod-product-compliance
Lightning Source LLC
Chambersburg PA
CBHW070845310526
45793CB00011B/592